T0055508

ABSTRACTS
AND BRIEF CHRONICLES
OF THE TIME

To my children, without whom never,
me

ABSTRACTS AND BRIEF CHRONICLES OF THE TIME

I.
Los, A Chapter

HÉLÈNE CIXOUS

TRANSLATED BY BEVERLEY BIE BRAHIC

polity

First published in French as *Abstracts et Brèves Chroniques du temps. 1. Chapitre Los,*
© Éditions Galilée, 2013
This English edition © Polity Press, 2016

Polity Press
65 Bridge Street
Cambridge CB2 1UR, UK

Polity Press
350 Main Street
Malden, MA 02148, USA

All rights reserved. Except for the quotation of short passages for the purpose of criticism and review, no part of this publication may be reproduced, stored in a retrieval system, or transmitted, in any form or by any means, electronic, mechanical, photocopying, recording or otherwise, without the prior permission of the publisher.

ISBN-13: 978-1-5095-0054-3
ISBN-13: 978-1-5095-0055-0 (pb)

A catalogue record for this book is available from the British Library.

Library of Congress Cataloging-in-Publication Data

Cixous, Hélène, 1937-
[Abstracts et brèves chroniques du temps. English]
Abstracts and brief chronicles of the time / Hélène Cixous. -- English edition.
pages cm
"This book is a chapter of The-Book-I-Don't-Write. It is the first chapter to have come along but, in the end, I'm almost sure, it will not be chapter one; among all the chapters none will be more first than any other ... " Introduction.
Includes bibliographical references.
ISBN 978-1-5095-0054-3 (hardback) -- ISBN 978-1-5095-0055-0 (pbk.) 1. Cixous, Hélène, 1937- 2. Authors, French--20th century--Biography. 3. Authors, French--21st century--Biography. I. Title.
PQ2663.I9Z4613 2016
848'.91409--dc23
[B]
2015022299

Typeset in 11.5 on 15 pt Janson Text by
Servis Filmsetting Ltd, Stockport, Cheshire
Printed and bound in CPI Group (UK) Ltd, Croydon, CR0 4YY

The publisher has used its best endeavours to ensure that the URLs for external websites referred to in this book are correct and active at the time of going to press. However, the publisher has no responsibility for the websites and can make no guarantee that a site will remain live or that the content is or will remain appropriate.

Every effort has been made to trace all copyright holders, but if any have been inadvertently overlooked the publisher will be pleased to include any necessary credits in any subsequent reprint or edition.

For further information on Polity, visit our website:
politybooks.com

TO MY READERS

This book is a chapter of *The-Book-I-Don't-Write*. It is the first chapter to have presented itself but, in the end, I'm almost sure, it will not be chapter one; among all the chapters none will be more first than any other.

There is a book I call *The-Book-I-Don't-Write* that I've been dreaming of for over thirty years. It is the master, the double, the prophet, almost the messiah of all the books I write at its call. This book precedes me and sums me up. It collects all my lives and all my volumes. It haunts and guides me.

I have often spoken of it to my friends. You know. It was always my promised book and therefore desired and despaired of, the shadow preceding each of my footsteps. I myself am the shadow of my shadow. Stendhal had to turn himself into a certain Henry Brulard to write his *My*

Life,* bringing together all the pieces of the life of Henri Beyle. One can only write the My Life Book by taking oneself apart and putting oneself back together, laughing all the while.

Jacques Derrida would say of this book: the one you don't write writes itself differently. I would have liked to see it one of these days before I die. I've renounced. It's the only thing I've ever wanted, the only thing I've ever renounced. It has never left me. It was like an immortal that has never known what it is to be born. I have never seen it face to face. I see it shining behind a veil, its indecipherable back, upright on heaven's bookshelf, its elegant silhouette, utterly foreign, utterly familiar, of future revenant. I've always thought it would come, naturally. When? After all my deaths? Just before, or just after, the last of my deaths.

Thus I've never had the eyes to see it face to face, the living, seeing eyes, able to look, without weeping, at all the visages of the Visage of god-the-all, otherwise known as *My Life*. (One understands why Stendhal in the guise of Beyle only thought about "his" "life" as *his* intimate foreigner.)

The Book that contained me, me and my lives, was with me, ahead of me, beyond me, walking like a misty, indistinct column, more myself than me, an all-powerful soul without an envelope, a too-naked letter, which I might almost have been able to read, but differently.

---

* *My Life*: in English in the original French text. Throughout *Los, A Chapter* words and phrases appear in English in the original French text. Most are identified in the endnotes but will not be signaled in the text.

These past few years, I no longer waited for it. I'd resigned myself. *That's when.*

It's always when, and only when, one has been through despair, which never stops hoping, and when one has acquired calm, that the absolutely Unexpected happens. That's when:

This book presented itself, all of a sudden, "one fine morning," all written, hovering just outside the window of my study, clearly constituted, like the at-term delivery of a dream from the head of a dream. Quickly, without taking my eyes off it, I copied it down, staying scrupulously close to its notations, its rhythms, its moments of silence. I found it. Just as you see it.

This is one petal of the Book-I-Don't-Write. A petal. Detached from the rest of the flower of the Book. *Los,* as my mother would say in her German language. *Los*: detached. That is, arriving: mobile: autonomous: destined. The instant of a life. An instant is always a present.

This is not a tale. It is *a today itself*, whatever its date, its action, its duration. It is a synchrony. A symphonic instant: it happens here-and-now, at top speed. Because of its condensation, its leaps, its eternal youth, because it hurries, like memory's revenant, one could take it for a dream. It is all true.

Car*los* is entirely true. Is an instant.

Every instant is equally the present.

It is a petal detached from the flower of my life.

The detaching happened by accident. The book-chapter-petal was torn off the flower by the violent blow of a death.

In truth, it owes its literary setting-free literally to

death. Life which gives death, or rather that rends it, this life born of death, might this be literature?

If Carlos hadn't died suddenly, dead of sudden death, carried away in an hour in time's river, the one that runs out, it might never have found itself alive in the world of petals of books.

Suddenly, that morning, I saw the universe of *The-Book-I-Don't-Write*: it is an infinity of presents. It is structured like a flower.

In this flower the petals are unnumbered pages.

The petal is also a flower. It is at once a page that is part of a structured whole and a separate individual, a flower of the flower.

My editor asks me if I already know what the next chapters will be. I see some of them, through the window, I say. Several are almost loose. They are already living, I sense. A gust of wind, not me, will decide, soon.

Hélène Cixous

Let them be well used; for they are the abstracts
and brief chronicles of the time.

Hamlet, Act II, Scene 2

The night I am prepared for mama's death I think I am losing her, I lose her, in the end she comes back, and as if in exchange that morning, to my astonishment, I find I have lost a friend, a friend more than a friend, a lover more than a lover, a comrade in adventures, I don't know how to say what he meant to me, what was, what is, tongue stammers heart too, who? who it is, kill, a great actor, a tactor, in which language to tell who, as we know from *Macbeth*'s second act, to kill to tell, there are only the *nors*, *Tongue nor heart*, carnage, the stuttering snore of impotence, I don't know which tense to choose to write a story cut in two halves, one dead the other resuscitated, I don't know what he is, was, will have been, will be, once from death incredibly resuscitated. So long as he lived, he was as if dead, I was tranquil, far from remembering, far from forgetting. He lived with me, Rue Lhomond. Yestoday.

To come back to my mother, on the 14th when mama warned me she was going to die that night, I hadn't, it seems to me, dreamed of him for years, I'm sure I hadn't feared for him, I now realize that I thought of him as immortal, someone I had no fear of losing, maybe he was inalterably conserved in one of those fate-free zones, where our near and dear whom fiction appropriates dwell dipped in golden wax, preserved in a cube of time that resists reminiscence and forgetting equally, he remained at 4 Rue Lhomond as in a palace of life, a Xanadu I must

1

have walked past a hundred times without stopping, as I pass but once a year Place de la Concorde, our sacred place, I even instinctively avoid going there, for fear I'll exhaust its golden charm,

I should call it the Sacred Place de la Concorde, or Saint Place, and drive by it just once a year, religiously, with your glittering ghost, my heart, at the wheel. One day I might draw a map of the world and indicate in gold the neighborhoods, shores, castles, cinemas, towers, restaurants, where our characters still live and breathe so strongly that I hear your being under the solitude, alive and hotly disputing beside me, your being though dead who never leaves me.

I was holding her hand, in the dusky room, I was laughing. She was saying: you laugh but I am not laughing. She was lying down. "I am scared of dying and you not being there. I feel the time has come. I am not laughing you are laughing. What are you writing?" I am writing what you are saying. "When it is time it is time. If I am going to die you weep. Now and then you look to see if I am still here." Half an hour later I stopped laughing, I was beginning to believe her. Mama doesn't tell fibs. This is the first time she has announced an expiry date. I see nothing. She sees something I don't see. When it is time it is time. A statement which imposes its pure authority. Now is the *hour*. She is faceless, soundless. The hour lures. A non-presence, a morsel of sly dry threadbare silence, a distraction, I should have known. I was waiting. Nothing. Thus she will play with me. I stretched a fine, discreet terror like a gauze across the room, the idea that I must not, could not not be at mama's side at the moment of no next moment. Here it is: you cannot bid each other farewell. This is the first time in my life that I am here at the same time as the time that doesn't come. I take notes. Mama speaks and speaks. She pours out all the thoughts and words she had set aside during this past year so poor in words. This rich supernatural dictation seems to end with the words: "You don't know what's going on. Whether it is tomorrow or today" – *seems*, for the next words: "best to fall asleep this evening," I didn't hear. An invisible fish feeling comes over me, I lean toward the sea,

Did I sleep? Did I die? I ceased. One loses consciousness before having lost consciousness. At a certain moment the past surpasses the present.

Next morning she is in full survival mode.

– *Was ist los?* says my mother. What's happening? What's not happening?

If death knocked, she was not let in. Probably she dropped by to take a look at her subject. We "sensed" her, if one can say one senses that one doesn't sense. *Los.*

Nothing surprises me any more, not life, not death, still everything surprises me, time has the form of an internal city, I live at several addresses, I have several selves to house, I visit myself diversely.

strange happiness, it is raining, this will be the first time we've made love in the rain, I tell myself, I let the Cemetery man walk away, quickly I join you. Your tomb not wet, no explanation. I put some lily of the valley atop your sex, more or less. I lay down on top of you. Take you in my mouth, as usual. Stand up, take me in your bones. Your voice hurries: Wait! Wait! I imagine him running through the hidden rooms, hallways perhaps. I wait. And here he is now, bright and clear despite his spectral cords which murmur our words close to my diaphragm. Isaac! I lick your ears, your toes, as fancy dictates. We are absolutely alive. We go off – generally you stay lit up in me for days – under a combative sun that tugs at clouds and bursts out laughing.

I lied during the night. When mama asked me: "What are you doing tomorrow?" I said: I'm going to see the eye doctor. I didn't say: I'm going to the cemetery to see Isaac. Telling the truth seemed to me violent. Soon I'll have several cemeteries to go and spend my lives in. I'm sorry I lied. It's as if I'd killed mama a little. After that, I said, I'll stay with you. Which is eternally true.

Mama has grown older since the 14th. I used to think she'd reached the oldest of old ages. I yield to the evidence: the work of aging is interminable. The parchment is each day re-devoured, re-freckled, oxydized, rusted. In the evening I kiss crusts of cheeks. A strange contrary life nibbles on the epidermis, rushes to keratinize each millimeter of what yesterday was called skin, and becomes moldy leather, pocked cloth. Someone in the cornered body won't let go. The flesh is in tatters, the thighs' ragged coverings are stuck together, adrift, having lost all memory of their function. The face is the scene of divided powers: all the traits, the caved-in structure, belong to the Great Rag and Bone Picker, but the eyes live on, sparkle, seek, are astonished, call, stay afloat. Nothing surprises me now: not life, not death. Meanwhile everything surprises me.

On the 15th the Radio quacks its morbid, colorless morning litanies, pours out its daily slop of cadavers, I lend it my deafness, vomit your bubble-wrapped catastrophes, whore of morning. Such is my indifference to its indifference that I don't take in a single sound.

That's when it comes

– A telegram for you. – A telegram? They still exist? – But *listen*! says the Radio. It's for you, the knife. Quit dodging it. – So hit me! I can't read. – You've received the blow already the haggard eye. – I did receive a blow, but I'm not sure, I don't feel a thing, was it me it hit? I fear it is. What does it say? – Shall I repeat? – Yes, yes, repeat, I want it, it's for me. – I repeat: "*Is dead. No last chapter.*" This time I wake up with a piece of my heart sliced off. Los: dead.

And at the corner where my two lives cross death a third soul quickly rises.

> *When love, with one another so*
> *Interanimates two souls*
> *That abler soul, which thence doth flow*

And in fifteen seconds you will hear the famous writer's name, the author of twenty-two novels,

6

canceled with a click, *The Iliad* and *The Odyssey*. The rumor is bruited: Homer himself has been struck from the universe. Others say "crossed out." Not Homer. Sterne, the divine son of the son of La Mancha. It seems he suffered, in another version, he seems not to have suffered

Tongue nor heart Cannot conceive, no, tongue is cooked, *cannot*, language stops, heart stops, what is happening, Macbethlennox Whatsthematter stutter in a single cut-off voice, the author is dead, tongue-nor heart-nor no longer able, my chest retches dry tears, a single sticky word remains to plug the hole: *Horror, orror, orro, ho* and it's Macduff who burps it or or or or is dead. *Los. Done.*

Unfortunately in the horrible dawn of which I am not the author, I don't shout Horror! Horror! Horror! Like everyone else, I would love to be able to vomit Macduff's naïve cries but in vain I search my chest for the sound that is equal to my fright. Instead of those noble childish words the midnight bell sounds its sad notes, "carlos is dead! carlos is dead!" O lovely horror tolls the midnight bell

And silently I cover up mama, who is freezing

– *Was ist los?* mama moans. – los – los –

– Los? What's that?

– We don't know. It is what we don't know.

– I thought it was Spanish. Isn't it?

– My love, I am consumed, I can no longer sign this letter except with what's left of

my name – Your Los.

– Have you read *The Book of Los?*

– No.

– NNo.

7

– *The Book of Loss?*
– No. *The Book of Los.*
– Ah! No.

Los is the name of the phantom, *ghost* or specter or
Gespenst or *fantasma* that has haunted mama for most of
the day. The thing that troubles us and doesn't answer.
– Do help me, love.

– *Los! Los!* o familiar vocable, so terribly familiar in my
mother's tongue, *Los*, sound of time, abridged, final note,
name of fate, *Los*, dio boia, butcher god, faceless prize, cry
of the ghost no one recognizes, I owe you a hymn in the
tongue of tongues,
   Lightning bolt-syllable,
   Cruel mask of the Event that tells us: No!

One thinks one is asleep, one can no longer imagine waking, the author having left before the end of the play, all is out one is all out, an atrocious sensation, everything has fallen down the Time hole except for the horror.

The world is Time's Wound

I dimly make out a violet pansy broken off Lethe's quay polymorphous, flotsam algae: what totally theatrical force, this thing that wears the mask called Death, it is the very essence of theater, the naked blow from the blue, the unseen Hand uproots the character that we have grown so used to being that we are it, yanks it up from the earthly stage like a carrot, and bites. In Chronos's mouth the carrot still cries: Horror! Orror! Gives its final cries, from between Chronos's teeth, a mush of living syllables, Carlotte, Carlos! For one dies in pieces, bite after bite one is taken, one is not blown out like a candle flame, raw and conscious the carrot dies, one has lots of time to feel dread. Blood's strong juice on the bitten tongue.

During the mortal chewing, during the tornado of swallowing, I have time and I remember. I remember the world, a minute ago, unsuspecting, my memory and I still remember the intact world, innocent of tragedy, so even after the news we live on, even dead we stillrelive, we live strongly, stronger, for a while yet, than death. It's not that I remember Rue Lhomond: I am there, I live there. Second floor.

Carlos lost: Carlos regained. Such is the strange theorem of resistance to nothingness. Nothing of what ceases ceases to be differently. Albertine is lost in order to come back, changed in a twinkling into cinematographic rays of light; Marcel's head heats to 39° on the average during the perpetual intermittent projection on all the surrounding surfaces, window panes, percale curtains, notebooks, doors. Another example: the transformation of *poor Lambert* (Stendhal writes *lantern* in the Henry Brulard manuscript, a marvelous, enlightening slip of the pen), twenty-five years after his death, into Saint John watching his friend and his God being crucified, which makes his friend Henry, who is both 10 and 35 years old, weep with ageless pain. I could fill six pages with *clear* memories. Not those wilted, mummified images one usually calls memories, but moments of life coming to life again, as in the theater where lives are re-enacted every day, with vigor, flesh, voices, life in no way different from real life, save for the calculated brevity of the incarnation.

They nail him in his coffin, they trundle him off, they bury him a few times: that's one way of looking at it, incontestably, the way of mortality. The heart, into which a nail is deeply driven, aches for quite a while. Later the wound goes to work. One energy is turned into another kind of energy. All we have to do is find within us the passive strength of the transfer: accept the transfiguration. And the mingling. A mingling of deprivation and

10

pleasure. Above all one misses the delights of the voice of the subject of this transformation. Yet the voice's particles are also changed into rays of light, the sound glitters and sparkles.

To come back to Carlos, what staggers me is the speed of his reappearance. No intermission between exit and the entrance. A quick change in the wings. I know all about this: behind the curtain the dressmakers pounce on the actor and while the audience is busy counting its tears and its palpitations, the actor, undressed, redressed, freshly made-up, re-enters, and the side of the heart that three minutes ago was wounded feels moved by a surprising joy.

What may surprise: when the change is so swift the heart spins, and the soul is darkened by a wave of guilt. This is what happened: Carlos's particles, annihilated, and then right away turning into rays of light. I feel: wonder, embarrassment; in the middle of my mental office, emotional chaos, the troubled sense that I have perhaps been tricked by some thieving sleight of hand, embarrassment, and finally wonder.

Later it comes to me that neither my desire nor my power of illusion is responsible for this quick change of energies, but rather the very nature of Carlos's particles. Los. His whole being was always busy transforming his own energies into wondrously diversified human material. So many individuals have been launched into the world's memory by his acts of imagination that he took his place ages ago among the small crowd of people cut from the fabric of mythology. In part fictional, these people are always already becoming renewable energy.

I think the sensation of the absolute, definitive, irreversible loss of Carlos exercised a firm empire over my being, for the space of one great day. I got a double jolt, that's what happened.

What to make of this scenario: when, for a first time, at the age of 8 or 10, my whole body shuddered at the idea of mama dying on me, and it was my father who died, there one day, not there the next. After that, every time mama was in danger, someone else died. You can think about this differently. When Isaac died? Same thing. No conclusion.

Everything happens while we are asleep. Last night I was wrong, I was struck down, I am dead, I was given a new life, there was a flash, and a solution was found in my absence. All of a sudden everything was taken from me, everything lit up. I was divided, I was put back together again. Lives that I'd neglected, years that I had left locked up in the next street and which had every right to believe they had been forgotten, came back to life, they came for supper, someone, I don't know who pardoned me, it was better than a pardon, it had the delicious taste of starting over – starting what over?

To believe. It's as if over time the unbelief got tired of nattering on the phone as she must so as to occupy the subject she suspects is tempted by belief – not to say faith. For, as opposed to faith, which doesn't speak, unbelief must resort to force to win and maintain its advantage. Which in the end results in its defeat. In all plays there comes a moment when we learn that we have never doubted the love we thought we doubted, or wanted to doubt practically our whole life; the flash of light is usually in Act V, either in the first scene or, more often, in the last, in which case it is too late, the Radio announces that King Lear's daughter has died at the age of 53. If an irate listener calls in for a correction, the Radio will answer I'll tell my boss. 53 or 35, what's the difference?

14

"I am going to be 75." Written in the Giacometti note-book this 16th of May. Long past, already. Next time in the chapter I'll be able to write: I am going to be 80. This is an old song, I could replace 75 by 50 or 85, according to the century of the publication of my thoughts, they can leave a blank space after "going to be," they can remove "going to" and "be," what it comes down to is I have five years left, whatever the century, just enough time. When Stendhal realized he was going to be 50 he summed his life up fast, a matter of minutes. I have just discovered my "fifties" etc., the rest is yet to write. Isaac received his fif-ties letter at 45. One always receives the fifties letter on the eve of a birthday. Carlos thought his letter came on the day he turned 40; he let out some big whoops, I was laughing, I didn't believe him, now and then I believed him, who knows I told myself, when I turn 40 maybe I'll shout too, Carlos's shouts were high-pitched and excited like the cries of a child that his Uncle Los, the bearded prophet, tosses into the air and threatens, with a chuckle, to let fall.

My letter came. I didn't shout – I didn't believe it. I looked around. The garden I love had a cemetery face. I can neither avert my eyes, nor believe them, nor lower my visor. I cannot tell myself what I am murmuring to myself. I love your cemetery face, o my life.

I heard they excavated William Blake's grave; all of a sudden the ground was re-landscaped, and nobody on the spot to say: Hold on! Let me gather up these bones. The crane snatched up all the letters, chewed up and spit out William Blake's atoms, and scattered even the dots that form the poems' letters.

What if my working days were numbered? On the 16th I tell my son: I have five years left. I see it: the book runs. It's as plain as the nose on my face. Already I can only see with my right eye. Urgent: I must tackle the book-I-don't-write. Before the 16th, I had been for years in awe of the vague, voluminous mass of "My Life." One doesn't discover. The discovery *happens* when one is not there, my son says. Exactly. *I* was not there. I, this me I'm attached to, on mama's orders, like poor Andromeda Proust to her rock. Blind by day and at night struck, as long as *I* live, by paralysis of the lower limbs, this me was not there.

– Five years, I say.

– Ten, my son says. Ten years.

– Three years, certain dreams tell me. Today is my birthday says the dream of May 18. I have a sudden urge to build an arbor in the garden. On the phone the gardener tells me: I'm good for three years. The man is my age. I am 53 (in this dream) and I feel the need to change, imagine, rearrange, act. The gardener fences me in: three years to write the Book.

According to the May 1 hyperdream, Isaac, you will have been given back to us for four years. That's good news. Four years of life, you and me, alone for one another, short but long, the main thing is you've come back to pick up your life. Enough to keep me going, *after*, till the end. I'll manage. A brief, but unlimited life, except for your frailty. You are ill. But active. Dashing, in your off-white summer suit. Today is our first day, Isaac. You are driving my car, since you came back with nothing. Empty hands, white suit. We'll go to the American University. To the Champs-Élysées of Proust, Ulysses,

16

Aeneas, an avenue to drive up every day. Kiss: mouth to mouth. In each other's arms, then: discretion.

– Because I will not always be able to, you know! Fatigued by death. – I know, I say. I say: I am happy. I absolutely am. It's enough to make the locked-up part of my heart burst. – Good, you say.

Four years of *life*: thus I will reach the age of 65 and be able to die. We kiss passionately in the elevator. A new life. What fun. – How's your mother? – Strangely, she's grown immortal. The fabulous turns real. The four years' grace transports me. Frail happiness. One can't take more than four years in the absolute.

The next day Carlos saw a rainbow alight on the front building. He took it for a sign. He was reading a Raymond Chandler book: "He's a genius. It's *The Odyssey*. I wish I could write like Raymond Chandler. I would feel fulfilled." His wish came true. The world in cothurnuses. He finished quickly, like a cup one drains.

"Carlos est mort." In French this is a present tense. Dead he lives. Dead, one lives a charmed life. Look at Isaac.

The Caravel goes down, in a single bound the pleasures and years pour out of the hold and land on my shore. The beach is a an untouched sandy fabric, a cloth of finest gold combed over hundreds of kilometers by the winds that chant in four languages on the shores of the Atlantic. His gaiety, his body half-naked on the bed, except for his notebook his mustache his glasses, his sonorous musical voice *Carlos died yesterday* and was resuscitated on Wednesday the 16th; his generosity is not generosity it is a natural elegance, the mustache of his mind, a fine line traced with a brush, his fears, his curiosity, his new trousers, his cries of fright at his birthday, cries-laughs, the crilaughs of the terrified blackbird that howls to scare away death; and its caterwauling does indeed scare off the cat, *forty is too many, no?*, his mocking fear of old age, his forever-ready lover's perfume, his rivers of visions, his triple sight, standing on the shore of Biscarosse, with Cortès and a young woman he calls Marina at his side, face to face with the giant breakers of the Ocean Orchestra, he orders New Spain's fleet to deploy its wings. We are on the verge of hallucination, the big-breasted clouds drip blood, his prophet's joyous sobs, next he writes his *Cartas de relación* in one burst of his firm and regular handwriting, what a marvelous contrast between the extraordinary violence of the cruelty he reports and the intrepid precision of the story he paints of it in blue ink. An army of five hundred men plus fifty horses, sticky with sweat and an outbreak of smallpox, manages to reduce a population of twenty-five million to a cemetery plot, likewise, although the subject surpasses Carlos by thousands of temples and events, the teller of the tale surpasses the subject, which rises, like the towers of Babylon of three continents, high above his notebooks and shuts him in a cage of magic paper. Carlos roars *Kill me as Woman, let me die / As a mere man.*

A peerless gourmand, his taste runs from the pear tart to his insatiable pleasure in inventing thousands of individuals every fourth day. You begin by imagining the person's family name, given name, age at the time of meeting; next you call this person in a strong, patient voice, then a Justo, a Peregrina, a Manuel, a John, a Doña Medea, a Rosaura, one or other, man, woman, from the great crowd standing on the quay behind time's curtain responds: Here I am! and steps forth into the circle of light cast by the desk lamp like a rug to welcome the still wobbly actors, and the improvisation begins with a dance step or two, the lightning bolt of love at first sight. I imagine the moment God looked at the other, his first love and therefore his last first love, with a ravishment full of longing for this creature: this is the last time he will see her for the first time, and so they gaze at one another as if this were a farewell! never again this brand new hour, so young and already dead. But there will be others and Carlos sits back down. Already the next creation's name comes to him. A transvestite, apparently, with two names. Carlos has a hard-on, and since he doesn't know for whom exactly, he bursts out laughing. The transvestite, Mimi to his friends, is shaped like a giant pear. Mimi is more than mysterious or mister. Mimi always looks earnest or giggly. You can twirl round them at top speed without producing the least oscillation. Mimi is welcome in Carlos's ark. Like a thick black curtain, his or her long straight hair drapes himher right to the equator. "If we lift the hair maybe we'll see an egg. A big egg," Carlos says. A tall and tranquil pyramid sitting on its big end in the middle of the quicksand calms the World's anguish. Lace cuffs the large hands. Four gold necklaces make a ladder that leads the gaze step by step from the ample breasts to the belly's circumference, and where the planet's stomach begins or ends no one knows, but no one has any doubt it contains the seeds of a new race.

Los is the self-creating prophetic imagination that broods in secret beyond good and male. In his mythology Los is himself the malefemale offspring of the author he is. Los is the name of the Eggchicken Blake created. My name is Los, the imaginactor says. Call me Ishmael, Los says. Call me Los.

Carlos, the name of Vautrin and Lucien de Rubempré's child, the proof that in books fecundation occurs between souls; as long as the desire is lightning fast this never fails to work. "The Love of Humanity," House of Shakespeare, masks and materials for every kind of theatrical production.

Those years when one may run into him pretty much everywhere, in Mexico City as at Paris Balzac, where he exercised his image-taming powers in mirrors, and even as master of mirrors for it is in the bedrooms, salons, mirror-guarded vestibules, that reality's creatures and those who live in books mill about, so similar, so different and yet almost all of them haunted by the spectacular surprises time deals out in passing to frail human creatures. Just as in reading I have always before me, among the irritable youth, the perturbed fathers, the family assassinations, resentments simmered to myth in the kitchens, on the one hand; on the other, the adulteries dangling in the bedrooms, in every closet almost without exception, the vision of Carlos himself traversed by the same astonishments, the same abortions of desires, the scars of passions that burned to the very same marrow as those individuals that he sends to their death, with or without regret, in his place, or for him, who are him. I'm almost certain that, myriad-minded, it is he who is incarnated in flashes in the passengers and guests of his imaginary hotels. The emperor of dreams. The whole troop of them. Welcome! The one who plays the king: him. The lover who sighs, the clown, the lady, the fool, the wild beast. Him. *Each actor on his ass.*

The Rue Lhomond is at the corner of the Rue d'Ulm, where the Rue Obregon crosses Lexington Avenue, not far from the Dôme du Panthéon. Abbé Lhomond, a simple man, dies in December 1794, without having been decapitated, without having had sexual relations. He is the author of one book: his Latin Grammar is his wife, daughter, son and his act of charity toward humanity, the gift of his solicitude toward all pupils poised on the threshold of secondary school who, for two hundred years, will have had a *Lhomond*, and to Carlos who finds a copy on November 8, 1968 in a bookstall along the Seine.

I tell my daughter: I was able to love totally and absolutely, simultaneously and unsimultaneously, two heroes at once; I believe I was able to love three people quasi-simultaneously. I've only ever loved Isaac, I say. This is all true. Everything is impossible, everything impossible is simultaneously and at every moment possible; it has to do with the street address where the impossible happens, with the hue of the passion, and often with the shape of the fingers and to be more precise with the shape of the beloved hand's fingertips, always ready to surprise.

When I loved A., I tell my daughter, I loved I., I. is the only person I have ever loved, all the same in a serendipitous life I loved A. passionately, I thought I was going to die but on the other hand it was impossible, I do not understand myself, I tell my daughter, I could list ten or twelve reasons for which I could or should have loved absolutely, simultaneously adored my friend and my god, this is the truth, still it sheds no light on anything. And so it goes.

I read, in Proust's handwriting, the line "she was dead" (page 83, notebook 54): the handwriting makes the words seem extra-alive, as if I were hearing the news from the hand of Proust, I hear it fifty or so times from notebook 54, and always, like him, for the first time, what a tenacious life this death, this corpse, has,

as for me, the minute I write "Carlos is dead," right away what life, what a racket, he wakes up, and what's more each time I say or write it, as if submitting to the Radio's lesson, he rises in the room so fast that the thought of death has never yet acquired the weight of reality,

it's as if I dared him, no way he'll let himself be caught. What an idea! Him, dead? He nips the nape of my neck. Grumbles.

As in a song, Proust multiplying melodic variations on the notes *Albertine*, *dead*, *reality*, *alive*, starting over a hundred times, because she, with all her strength, resists. That's what "dead" is. The word may be in the newspapers or on the internet, but not Rue Lhomond, not in Biscarosse, not in Prague, not in New York, I'm not denying the threat, but the days when his being was so alive are too well preserved, by me, in me, I cannot conceive that they may crumble to dust in me, my flour rises,

that of those days lived so meticulously I will never manage to say: "those days ~~themselves~~ became themselves the past and their ~~ash~~ decomposition ..."

26

not that I refuse to lose, or to share the common lot of mortals. But it is C. Los the being himself whose alchemical formula resists annihilation.

With my own eyes I saw him transform his entire person into fabled personage. His plans were laid.

And you, what is your name in this story? Call me *It All Depends*.

Depends on Tyger Burning: Bird, Blueblack Bird. The day C. calls him Ash. He laughs. You can get high on Ash. C. devours the confessions of opium eaters. And wakes up tygerbird. Concoction: stir two souls together with a mix of animal souls.

According to Isaac your name is Montagne. This surprises you. Aren't you a grain of coffee? – You are a montaigne. That's life, that's the aim, the summit, the climb. You are also a grain of coffee in a ship loaded with spices.

According to Montaigne, his essays are like peat formed from a material that is light and resists rot, a millenary compost heap. Peat can smolder for years. It doesn't soil you. It powders you. According to Los, Blake reports, ecstasy is the color of violets.

When? November 24, 1968. *Lola Montès* in the violet cinema Le Styx. The topic, in the restaurant Le Voltaire: why a writer stops writing. To my left a faceless old maid in a silk dress sups alone with herself and the past. Crudités, turbot sauce suprême. White and thin, out of a Carlos novel. Damp plants start to climb the table legs. The waiter, small, waist cinched by a corset, girlish gestures, wears a bracelet with his name on it: Arlette. Offers a light. Lolarlette.

Taxi for the Cuban Embassy, Paris wet, empty, Saturday night, Avenue Foch, the smell of the building.

Cameras roll.

Madame Carpentier opens the door. Circus of the Degenerates. Sugary-smelling men, stiff-legged women whose bellies stick out, with big tight arched buttocks.

– Can you picture Carlos without a mustache?

– Without a mustache I'm horrible, I am like a big naked buttock wearing glasses.

Letting the words fall on the floor, Carpentier, gloomy, flesh sagging, announces, I have to write a cantata for four hundred choristers for tomorrow I shall get up at four a.m. Voice toneless.

A gang of frenetic, hooting little girls goes by, does ring-a-round-a-rosy in a room whose double doors yawn at the hall.

A petite young woman in trousers, visibly proud of

29

her normal-sized but in comparison singularly small buttocks.

Musicians. A sprinkling of blondes. Plates of rice strewn here and there on the ground. Olive oil salesmen, kinky-haired presidents. Short, with rickety legs. The hideous suits. In a corner a TV set scorned by all. From time to time someone winds up the daiquiri machine.

In comes the little Venezuelan, puppy dog in big glasses, his motto: have another drink. Effusions. Looks at the camera, me, head tossed back.

Conversation: Carpentier-Carlos seated on rocking chairs. Let's talk man to man. My mistress decided to leave me yesterday. It's final. What should I do? Carlos has no idea.

Conversation with Saura. Who are you? A Spanish painter. I make my living painting. What do you do? No idea. Someone else. Would you like a daiquiri? No. An intellectual. What a pity. I'm going to fetch you a daiquiri. Yes. While he waits I fetch my coat and leave.

May they be well treated. *For they are the abstracts and brief chronicles of the time.*

Night Avenue Foch taxi a calm return. Dance of the buttocky Cuban women, hot men, guitars, upside-down rocking chairs, daiquiris, pity. Nude lone universe.

Cut.

Sleep. Gratitude. I tell my daughter I am ready to die. I know everything. My daughter, dressed as a boy, can be my companion. We ascend the Mythological Staircases. Pure, wide, empty steps that can take us to every exit: desert, sky, endless road, grotto of the sirens, mountains, islands. In my haste I put on only a simple sleeveless dress, no panties. Let's hope nothing happens. My daughter: how well you read the Bible. It's Ovid's, I say. I dip the Bible in gold powder, mimosa semolina in a pretty round dish. We taste it. My daughter: "This bible flour is so Cixous." Appreciated. I appreciate. Gratitude. Suddenly Carlos. Noisy. Far off. I dig a hole.

Camera!

Farther on. My body wrapped in Isaac's hardness, my soul asleep, distant. Mouth full of bible. Carlos's hands on the slender subject. Ovid, Book 1. Skin of oleander wood. Two hands. One to hunt love, the other to fan it to life. *Sagittaria duo tela pharetra: fugat hoc, facit illud amorem.* I smile. *Delius hunc viderat adducto flectentem cornua nervo: quidque tibi, lascive puer, cum fortibus armis?* Delius had seen him man his bow, strings drawn taut: what do you need such a potent weapon for, you little rascal? She seeks to soften the bark round his chest, but the hardness of Isaac's arms around her. Alas! What have I done? Three months I have loved him, I loved him, I would have loved him today I'll have him, and tonight laurel

His naïveté, his egoism, his gaiety, whatever he wants

31

he thinks he has, tricked by his own prophetic words *sua illum oracula fallunt*, his Achilles' heel: his godlike coarseness, enormous terrors, tender excitements. Slippery little kitty, slow now go slow, I don't want to hurt you his arms enlace the branches, he kisses the barky thighs. Quick, his hand between the thighs *oscula dat ligno*, he moans, he kisses the bark, his long fingers go in. Why is your cunt so sweet? My cunt is not sweet it is not my fault, it was all written, my body attributed, stubborn strong guardian of passions worked out in another book, *Primus amor*, first love and first book. Steep walls, narrow gorge, I'm too far from myself. Virgo intacta, but penetrated through and through with love, with loves. Whose fault? Then the Delian falls onto her, groaning, the body electric burning bright, quick furious shudders in the forests of the night, his hands at the slender woody throat. How innocent we are, how poorly separated, blissful hence provisory, struck by contradictory arrows.

Where? very far, over there, in another chapter written in one go yesterday like a reality still strange to her, that fights me despite me, against Isaac's tindery body. Whose hands are at your neck, what shoulder and what art could twist the sinews of thy heart, and in what language does it beat, the heart that knows not who flees who to flee, the one in hope the other into a dim future. My neck hurts, the one sure thing, bless it. The hands squeeze my shoulders my arms, and what dread hand, and what dread feet little by little the idea that a poem can become real when it discovers in what vigorous being it may be sown and take root, these taut thighs clamp these legs, crush the calves' pulp, are really and truly the limbs forged for Tyger on Blake's anvil. I'm going to strangle you, he roars. In French. Joker! But he began to strangle me. I was dreaming that Carlos had fallen onto me like a god heavy as a tree and drunk and that he was strangling me with his naturally supernatural hands. My neck hurt. Under my right ear my jaw was nicked by a bite. Please mister Tyger! More firmly: Tyger! Don't do that! I dream that I am dreaming this. Still, you have to protest. Without conviction I say, please big mister Tyger please don't strangle me. The sentence gets crushed in my throat. A jolt, some pressure, to my surprise I choke therefore I dream, I try to speak I dream that I am not dreaming that I am dreaming that I am going to die in this strange manner and *it is really real*. Fistfuls of sentences drop like torn-up scraps of paper. Bite, don't kill me. Don't do that! Did he who made the Lamb make thee? In vain one bleats. The sinews of my back vibrating from his teeth in my nape. And suddenly you surrender. Why not, after all? A strange story. Everything is resolved. I accept. I renounce. She is dead. Is she dead? Mister Los curls up moaning and trembling in his corner. Illusion? A real tyger in the bedroom.

Cut! Carlos views it. Something has escaped him. It is too soon. More *sawed up*, Carlos says. I think I under-stand, I think. I cite Stendhal's scenario: Henry madly in love to the point of popping a vein at the very mention of a *saw*:

My sweetest effusions with my friend took place while he sawed at the woodshed, separated from the courtyard, at C., by an open partition formed of walnut uprights turned on a lathe, like a garden balustrade.

L. Place where Lambert used to saw logs for my

grandfather's fireplace. – H. Me. From here I would contemplate the wooden bars of the shed and give myself paroxysms of pain by opening my mouth and letting the blood rush to my head.

That's it exactly. Place where Lambert used to saw recalls place where Doctor Frankenstein dreams of remaking a body for his beloved assassinated. One must be frankly fantastic. I still have the shards of Carlos's delighted voice in my ears.

Back to the beginning.

Small, narrow room, almost abstract. Hopperish frame. Head toward the door, feet toward the window. Camera's point of view: in Carlos's sketch the two characters seemed to have embarked in the flying coffin of a tale out of Wagner for its theatrical exaggeration, out of Buñuel for the almost droll ferocity of its eroticism. Even stronger, more frightening, more troubling, the violently dreamlike scene:

[Long gallery with elegant small windows. – Lavatory reserved for the family. – My uncle's room. – Woodshed. – Spinning tops – T. My grandfather's thermometer. – L. Place where Lambert did the sawing. – How he placed the log. – Rope. – Saw's teeth. – C. Saw's rope. – R. Piece of wood to stretch the rope tight.]

Bed in which he was sawing. In this bed Montagne played the lamb with T.

I don't remember.

In this bed Montagne played the lamb with Isaac. Same bed, or almost. Small elegant windows. Woodman! Something is burning! Quick change of soul. Burn me, Isaac! I have only ever loved you. Text.

– Who's this T. in your texts? asks T. Asks Isaac. Says Carlos. Tell me tell.

– T.? Thee.

35

– You can laugh, but I'm not laughing.
– I'm not laughing: I'm writing.
– Never ask who for whom. It tolls for thee.

Close-up: hands. Mascufeminine. Do they seem to breathe? They breathe. Moan. Move, opened, closed, wing cases of scarabs.

Isaac's fingers, short, the nails trimmed square, a mason's or a carpenter's broad palms, fingers to join, screw, tame matter, and therefore as if grafted on a mind millions of vocables are coursing through, active as electric particles. The workman that Isaac might, in another version, have been. In the case of Carlos, where one expects paws with powerful claws he has long slender phalanges, proof that his inner child hid a girl still play-acting Antony Cleopatra. Both of them together in the contretemps. Every day this astonishes me afresh.

Carlos looks at himself in the glass. He rewinds his age. Back to when he let his mustache grow for the first time, back, back to the Jungle. Back to *The Songs of Innocence*. In his head he sees himself in London in 1788. Back to *The Book of Los*.

Isaac looks at himself in the mirror, in the elevator especially, he checks himself. Here and now. – What time is it? – End of Juventus, beginning of old age.

I look at them looking at themselves.

I look at me looking at them. Isaacarlos. Carlisaac.
They are looking at their ghosts. Asking their doubles to
be faithful. Horror of the hourglass.

Back to the beginning. Carlos is an important character in the Book-I-Don't-Write. As vital to it as Stephen Dedalus, Bloom, Raskolnikov, little Kolia Krassotkine, Albertine, Akhmatova, Piotr, all the theatrical beings who inhabit the streets of The Book and whose familiar silhouettes I can feel shine at my windows. My mental family. To mention but a few. Murder or suicide is in the air. The scene of "the end" concerns them. Like "one of the fine arts." They all think of death, each awaits it differently. I nourish them all with its marrow, its hair, his secrets. At times C. is the main character, it all depends what mood the chapter is in, if it's War, Peace, or both, or time to write so as to wonder, while wondering, what makes one write, what makes one stop writing, sometimes.

Carlos, Los, C., C. Los, Carlisaac, so many names, you never know from one sentence to the next what the book will call him.

He sleeps in this bed, his high brow helmeted in mistrust, closed, off-limits to all gazes but his own. Carlos in the inner cinema. A gigantic full-length Antaeus, hard and wise, his mouth glued to his mother's belly, all earth, all woman. He touches her only to distance himself from her. Take so as not to be taken. He chooses the moment, chooses the instant of exit, of the embrace, the waking, the conquest, the defeat. Unaware that he chooses. Didn't choose to choose. Everything decided in the flash of its conception. "My adored son," his father's sighed words, whereupon he is born adoredson. With a train of fabulous ships. Conquistadored. Masculinefeminine till the stroke of midnight. The sun, four hours up, is waiting?

Let it wait: Montagne doesn't touch him. No touching during his sleep. There is, in Montagne, a shrewd old soothsayer, an octogenerian Greek, well concealed under the face's three thousand years of unchanging youth. Here the son commands, the father adores, Montagne watches over them. Burly, with his shield of bronze skin, the hero calculates the simultaneous waking of all his limbs. No body part is to be surprised by a *she*. She: Montagne or solitude. The powerful-elastic body, lover of the air that knows to carry him without possessing him, gathers its forces for the leap. The camera crouched, still. Hup! Action! One might be filming "Albertine Sleeping" in 1922. Proust does not want to let go. He broods over her. A vulture.

– Hello you little sparrow, bluebird, blacksun, goldeng-
     Cut!

What separunited them: Carlos knows Montagne knows you must not tell what you know on pain of losing the knowledge's secret force. C. thinks only of nourishing the book that is writing him. The book is the beast in the jungle and the jungle is C.'s consciousness kept savage and virgin, the beast is his art's secret. Carlos prowls. Montagne's sexually ambiguous mind snakes through the forest of living pillars. Baudelaire sucks at De Quincey's male breast. The hallucinogenic milk circulates between the beds, the drinkers have dreams that last for two hundred years each night, you go to bed in 1822 you awake in 2012, I seem to have lived a millennium this night, maybe it is 2968 outside.

His hair raked back, mustache sleeked, he discovers:

She stands, bent, pale, in a trance, eyes turned inward. She is not looking at him. She gazes at death to come. Mesmerized. Watched by the sovereign's heavy lids. Not a word, stock still

– You look like a Piero della Francesca this morning.

Right away regrets having said it. But there is still time to touch up the painting that she is, he fears, about to rob him of, he is sure of it. He says: You know it. She says: I know. It's the neck. She bends her neck to Solomon.

– No, it's all of it, the neck, the profile, the bones, death showing through youth. No, it's the old man I had in mind. An old man, but it's you.

Better suspend the sacred conversation here. Solomon is rising. Sheba descends.

She knows that fast arduous worried brutal attentive at this very moment he is arranging the images of the scene the book awaits, it will be read later, when they no longer exist, she he held from 1492 to 1968 or a hundred years on, as this day in his arms, grazed by the rusty brown white hair of his arms, a tortoiseshell feline, in the little torch-lit room which smells of the children's hair, where he weaves where she recalls, becomes, is, the old man in profile, with his tanned skin, who surmises and doesn't say which of them has the greater pleasure.

The centuries pivot, she descends on the other side, following her equivocal dreams, walking upside-down as they liked to believe the peoples of the other side did.

And descending toward the wellspring of time, she grows older clothed in black velvet, her face sporting the mask of the inscrutable half-smile.

A blueblack bird's feather, alone, dropped, unique, lying on the carpet of leaves dead and alive, twenty-five-meter-high ferns: on the whole vegetal continent the sole animal presence. Nothing less carnal, nothing more spiritual, promise, messiah. Long thin greyblue. A clue. An angel's pen. Nothing more exciting. Sparrow specter. It smells of bird armpit. One smells it, licks its quill, its barbs, it quickens, irritated one seizes it by the throat flings it in the air, gives it back its lost flight, one admires its svelteness, synecdoche, its slenderness, its elegance, the feather more elegant than the bird, it spins, it twirls, makes Tyger tremble from his muzzle to the tip of his tail, one tires of it, it lies weightless, without energy, detached, passive, out-of-breath remains of an airplane life, funerary feather among the yellow leaves. Guess what? They found Pangea the earthly archi-continent, a vegetable Pompei. In Inner Mongolia. On its giant carpet, a feather. One can reconstitute the bird. Emotion of seeing this tall brightly colored ghost. Three hundred million years separate me from myself. We too existed.

Between flesh and mind there is a door that opens onto the depths, the shameful parts of one's art, the place where it stirs up the erotic transmutation of the worlds it has seized hold of. He takes the door and bangs it. Ay-yi-yi! Montagne cries.

Consultation. Isaacarlos, timidaucacious, in the elevator mirror: – How do you like my image, my sister? Montagne: – It never changes. I.: – Am I still 34 years old? I fear time's voracious speed. Am I white or am I black? M.: – Black for eternity, each time you are in the elevator. Your age depends on where you are in relation to me such that I see you as you wish to be seen. I.: – I would like to be able to see myself as seen by you. M.: – I keep for ever this inner image of You at 34 Years of Age utterly natural, deeply invariant, independent of any vicissitude, and which is You-Yourself, You at the moment T where the axes of your life are parallel to the axes of your being, in H, in the Helevator.

Isaac wants to believe Montagne. He gives his hair a furtive comb in the mirror so that the axes of his life align *exactly* with the axes of his self. And at this moment, whatever he is, he sees that he is 34. Even if he is 50, 34.

Isaac believes Montagne. Totally (illumination and grace) each time and the entire elevator time. What luck you live on the fifteenth floor! Absent the elevator the front seats of a car modeled on the little divan in their bedroom replaces the sacred cell. The little divan is itself a metaphor for life speeding by, a flying chair in which they make love all the more wildly as the vehicle is uncomfortable. They grab each other's ears, genitals, all the body parts are sexual organs toes mouths thumbs, to avoid falling separately, they acrobat like pro tem gods, both awkward and at the same time exceptionally gifted monkeys they exchange the whole and the parts. These moments of coincidence when one is in touch with eternity on earth are brief but in the space where memory and imagination wed they know no corruption. Montagne numbers and records them in a notebook. I have just made myself come by reviewing one (number 43, chosen at random, in one of my exultation notebooks) hatched forty years ago.

Dawn of a birthday. A flight of arrows. He cries again and again, like a cock alarmed by morning. Next Carlisaac heads to the bathroom, to curiosity, a face-to-face, good sports, both of them, horrified, but he examines himself in the mirror, with his Spallanzani glasses, Hoffmann's optician, the player is handsome, no? Supple, the eye bright. I am forty, it shows, it is visible, all things considered he is not unhappy with his inner image, all by himself he is forty, forty actors, inventors, thieves. With such a talented troupe of actors, he can reasonably hope to create the Human Comedy of the Occident and the Orient. Each of the forty can act three or four roles on the average, forty times forty characters, it's doable. At this particular moment, his life, his looks, his loves, all times forty, align with his self. Montagne sees him emperor and full of fears. Little fears good for taking the mind off the big fear of dying.

Fear of dogs, of airplanes, of driving, of women, of removing his boots while traveling. Of the double chin in the offing.

Voluptuousness of being thought, told, looked at, seen. Volupterror. – Why do I want to destroy you? I want disaster. Disaster. I want le mot en français. Disaster. Des astres, non? Kill the images. Save the visions. Shut your eyes or I'll put them out. She glitters glances. Man, I shoot. Woman, I melt, face bloodied, neck clean. Man bends, kisses the neck. He puts this into one of his fantastic tales. He crushes a sparrow in his hand. Ouch, these bones prick! Who'd have thought a little bird could have such sharp bones? She has trouble reading the tale: believes it. The fledgling murder. Convinces herself the horror is only a dream. She has seen worse. She doesn't remember. He dreams worse. To the point of bursting a vein. To write. So was it true, that dream?

That very day they love and don't love each other, out of love they don't love they avoid each other not loving whenever they reach the well-lit rooms right away you know you must merge with the shadows into which saint and fauve vanish, even if you must stripe your back with fearful symmetries as red as red meat, oodles of blood, of all kinds, you look for the cut, you slash yourself from side to side half the heart during the night, like the mystics, during diurnal love you twine your arms with curves, that's love

crazy the speed at which they drive an armchair down the carnal highway that was supposed to go to Prague in flames and has just passed Orléans, the non-driver is at the wheel, the countryside sweeps by like greased lightning, signs tell anyone listening the various ways into this story, they receive many letters, she notes all the signifieds, but the time to read and shout: Oh, so that's what this is all about! is still in the distance. Slow down! Slow down! they shout to one another. Whence an acceleration. Filthy love! Who knows when this will end how humanly. For who can remain supernatural (and if not all god, at least up to one's breasts) for more than three years?

– It's her whose tongue slips. Him, the cathedrals of wet sand.

I am Dante in America.

Why does Montagne see C. Los so much bigger than all kinds of objects standing alongside him? Because she sees C. Los and the objects at the same distance whereas they are not.

Standing facing the Ocean's giant breakers, observing the fleet's movements from the dune, he looms in her eyes as large as a general so passionately overestimated by himself in the first place, and hence by his lover and then by the secretaries, the captains, the rival emperors, the hyped-up friends, by Cortázar, by Enobarbus, the public hallucinates a hero of supernatural dimensions. He sees himself straddling the Atlantic Strait. Antony-seen-by-Cleopatra. With a few kingdoms he fashions her a throne. She changes Egypt into a nation of postal workers. No sooner does he read one letter than the next one turns up. They hold the world in their hands. As long as the film lasts the magnification keeps the spectator in an intoxicating state of levitation.

All of a sudden Montagne realizes he is standing in front of the Ocean as if it were a mirror, he sees himself as Ocean.

They film the scene *My man of men* on the beach at Biscarosse. They film a toy sailboat very close up, pummeled by the wind and half-swamped by a bucket of water. The smaller it is the bigger it seems. A. Shakespeare knows all the tricks.

A sheet of paper.

You draw a stick figure on the beach: C. You see the ocean. Because he is standing in the foreground, C. fills half the page. You draw the horizon line at the level of his chest. On the horizon line, draw a three-masted schooner, much smaller than the man, because it is very far away. Should it approach the coast, it will be impressive. How miniature the monumental is at such a distance! This touches you. The three-master is called *Antony-and-Cleopatra*, you muse, seen from afar. Remember the terrible ship that fled and precipitated Antony's downfall?

Now you erase the horizon. Erase the dividing line that shifts between sand and sea, in order to merge the man in the foreground with the background and its boat. Draw a string from the man's hand to the ship's mast.

A piece of string and he (Carlos) grows as big as the cosmos.

Eventually I saw the Spanish fleet arrive. Telepathy's pressure is irresistible. Even skeptics bend under the mystical blast.

Each time I return to the empty beach at Biscarosse I see the perfect illusion setting sail for Havana; silver sails edging the horizon and, carried through the crystalline air, the powerfully invisible strains of *My man of men*. Coltrane. A phenomenon which to this day has never failed. July 2014.

How short a century is. A few pages of notes. A hundred years of entries and exits dates births and deaths, my deadfather is born, from there I enter page 1914 Giacomo Joyce, today page 2014, "today" page 2114,

same miniature epic grandeur, the subject is about to die,
he renounces all but the writing.

– No?
His way of asking for a yes.

Have I been? This indeterminate stranger *femmeman* monk munchkin this ephebe with the claws of an ibis, this let-her-being who poems all the letters the parts lost crossed stubborn that dog earth and sea and in the end discourage discouragement for twenty years and counting of postal destiny; you must admit that nothing outlasts these frail and ultra-resistant messengers. Unknown to herself who walks at times with her wings folded, who flies at times somberly, who tries to take too-narrow streets. Her car rushes in, the street starts to strangle her, Prague, abandon the car, adieu, lord so dear to my heart. *Vale et ave.* You jump on a bicycle whose slim sky-blue-lacquered frame makes its way without mishap right to the top of the hill and *there*: the promised century you will not enter. Will I have been?

I have, to be sure, inherited her archives. For the rest, she is foreign to me.

I never hugged Carlos while keeping a space between us, so as to see him step back and take his place in eternity

I did not try to see him as I had seen him long ago for the first time for ever other and already in that instant unforgettable

I did not see him for the first time, I did not want my eyes to hold onto the forever-threatened image

I did not want my eyes to hold onto the hour of the first face

no beginning, no final scene, no catastrophe, no anniversary, no suffering.
– No separation? No poison, no dagger, no burst of machine-gun fire?
– Not with Carlos. With Isaac, yes.

On July 25 he has a sudden urge for a new pair of trousers. His body is the world. Each desire is the image of the big Desire: time's festival, celebration of the race, animal (lamb? goat?) "sacrifice on life's altar. The trouser desire: wild, irrepressible, he needs, he needs, he wants, if not to be condemned, then led blindfolded to a seedy hotel. Wants – since when? Since yesterday, more and more, a night and a day, a pair of pants the chief protagonist of these revolutionary days?

A nice nubbly off-white linen that espouses his thighs, stronger than any desire, stronger than the desire to desire the New America. Raw, *greggio*. The pants above all. Whose "cut" he loves.

A good cut. As soon as he saw them he knew. The pair he was looking for. Side pleats white, waistband like cool arms squeezing his hips, love without having to make it. A slender fabric hand without fingers, firm on his sex.

– Am I circumcised? – Yes. – Velours? – No! Velours broadens. Silk. The silk of the self. *You castrating bitch.* Velours gives, loosens, like the body of a woman when he's having his way with her. Whereas canvas shrinks. But he needs a size 33. One more day. An extraordinary pain shoots through his thigh. Trace of a recent burn. Montezuma's ferocity again. Unreeling its uprisings, history rushes in where it can. A night and a day July 25, 1522 of 1968, shadows of helmets, tank hulls. They leave fifty men and two cavalry at Tascalteca. A more significant and stronger city than Grenada and Algiers combined.

While he waits for the size 33 he devours his flambéed kidneys convinced that here from all eternity is a crossroads between (1) the kidneys, and more exactly those of the restaurant at 68 rue des Saints-Pères, cousins all unawares of the kidneys of June 16, 1904; (2) his neighbor, a face-lifted old flirt who murmurs to a little fascist all my friends tell me I look like Garbo; (3) the mysterious weight of the wars erupting like buboes along all the coasts of a beautiful continent making terror and pain reign over all the days of a present that goes on howling under torture, and withdraws in a flash like a dream decamping at five o'clock in the morning, a carnivorous thief who robs the dreamer of a city where some five hundred thousand people lived, in whose market one found clothing, shoes, gold jewelry, feathers, pottery of all sorts, wood, medicinal plants, places to shear goats, at five past five nothing remains, along the coasts the great grey backs of bunkers stare at other oceans, the heavy eyelids of fears, fear of oneself, fear beyond, bearing witness for no one, for no one comes here any longer, here where populations trembled and died, only the name remains; (4) and the creation of a human comedy, a divine comedy, or an archi-capital that no horrible accident will ever be able to efface from memory's membrane.

– Apple tart, it too flambéed. That's when: blingbangcrash a police car collides with the Saints-Pères, shouts ring out, the car explodes in flame and all, it was awful, wasn't it? – "Reality?" – Yes. It proves that Balzac exists.

TheWholeCity (Parisberlinnewyorkrome …) is The Globe Theatre Cinema where future ghosts and statues mingle, the officious ghosts and the specters of those who were alive only in their imagination, and who therefore are never dead, who beat all the records, who teach folly, thus infinity, to us, we little finites who are stronger than all their genitors together, more brilliant more creative than the society of creators, and all nonetheless shadowed by the melancholy shadow of which they are the outcome. Photo: Julio Cortázar, Oliveira, Luis Buñuel, in the Café des Deux Mondes, with Nikolai Stavrogin, Don Quixote. Copyright Los La Sybille. 1969. All of them are now seated around a table in the Café des Deux Mondes. Undated.

No matter who you are your days are numbered. Three hundred million years in a wink. Who knows what "a long time" means? It changes all the time. Voodoo words. Someone makes himself a name. There's a tribe where all the men are called Longtime, or maybe it is all the women. Each of the City's inhabitants has the right and the good fortune to bask in a few moments of eternity: it suffices to find oneself wide awake in X, with one's *self* open to the event on the one fine day when the axes of our life form an angle with the axes of world History. It was my good luck to be on the right path in X in 1968 in 1981 and in 1983. Three moments of painless lightning that occurred Place du Panthéon in Paris, though at somewhat different places. In 1968 I was walking toward the Rue Lhomond with the monument at my back. In 1981 I stood on the right facing the building with Isaac behind me. In 1983, I was walking down the Rue Soufflot in a demonstration when A. walked up it toward me. These three Invariants of Eternity might have happened elsewhere. Some whole-cities, like certain sacred places (woods, grottoes, temples), cast an *unheimlich* spell over their future ghosts. They attract, intoxicate, dissimulate their fine cemetery bodies behind their howls of laughter.

Not airplanes, which leave Earth in their wake. In 68 he likes the railway station, the City's perineum. If the world over here is rotting, he heads over there. Get away from the immobile peoples. Train, the unpredictable. He is the train. *Le train, c'est lui.* These days Rossinante calls herself Carriage.

Back from Prague: "When I left García Márquez we agreed everything was going to the dogs, we wept, the times call for tanks, the world is about to blow up, no? Then I hopped on the train and began to laugh." And the world bounded onto the quay. Bonded? Had a boner?

Seen, by Carlos, the sun, snow, Barcelona, are true: Bruegel, Piranesi, Picasso.

Trash talk. Seen from the Styx with its purple armchairs with Carlos alongside, Hercules is Samson whom Milton exalts and sobs over in lines that surpass him, praise him to the gods. *To outhamlet hamlet you have to outjesus jesus.*

According to the Kabbalah, in 1968, Year of the Tank, there were wisps of prehistoric animals in all the skies of the universe, I haven't forgotten. I have forgotten. The frothy month of Mayjune goes on and on. We film *Z* in Algeria on Moretti Beach. I have completely forgotten. In Paris only ice cream and cake are selling. And perfumes. I forget why. Covered with graffiti, wall art gasps and dies, that I do remember. Mayaugust one torrential day. I see: C. Los in a white suit up near the Lyçée Louis-le-Grand transfixed by a commando of urinators. To think that in France you can kill a State with ridicule. Meanwhile in Greece the actor who plays the god is killed, and eviscerated.

Fuck as you like. But seriously who has time to fuck? Latin American exiles hop on trains for Europe. They buzz around. Their hive is at the bottom of the Rue Saint-Jacques, Café La Bucherie in the Fifth Arrondissement. Rendez-vous at Joyce, on the terrace: one of those you-had-to-be-there nightmares of History.

No one reads for three months nonstop these days except the ghost of Shakespeare and Company. A plague the Bible did not include in its Egyptian lists, so improbable it seems. One doesn't read one isn't read.

One is adrift in an undated chapter of *The Odyssey*. We descend from Calderón.

In humanity's caves there's a cruelty that bubbles freely only in dreams. Hearts yanked out, hanged men eviscerated alive. Calderón writes *Life is a Butchery* with the blood of his dogs and darling cats, he slits their throats on the paper, begs their pardon with gushing tears, next we nibble on their lamb cutlets in the Restaurant.

Hence the white suit.

All beings without exception circulate in the form of atoms of dreams, giblets of signifiers, swirls of syntax, in the wings of the greatest play in the world dreamed by the dreams of dozens of artists disturbed in the construction of their major oeuvre, and urgently mobilized to weave a sort of wounded Babel in holograph gauze. Their historical period, their language, their particular domain are of no importance, only their extravagances are required, they dream with their regiments of heroes and divinities on board, and all kinds of heartrending sounds, tolling bells, volcanic eruptions, snoring squadrons, but also siren silences, silences. Muffled voices on the telephone. Coming from so far away that you feel you hear Cape Horn groaning in the Saint-Michel metro station. The whole day echoes with clarion calls from all the ages of copper. You are startled.

This is a story with no anniversary, I tell my daughter. It can happen at any moment or repeat itself. The events of 68 can be replaced by the events of 81 or by others from 2001, the figures could be 18, 19, 20, 21, 48, 70; our travels will be toward countries struck with this or that plague, the trajectory of Ovid or of Mandelstam will be forever traceable, one will dally with Armenia or Argentina, one will flee Florence or Athens or Cuernavaca, one returns, one meets up with the other revenants for a drink. Sometimes everyone is alive. At others everyone is gone. The survivors get together in Strasbourg: Goethe shows you round the cathedral. From the bell tower one sees the whole city of Europe.

Europe, purveyor of souvenirs to the world. Where poets drop anchor; where their dead bodies are, their bars, their hotels, their tombs their youths. The gilded skulls of the monuments. A marketplace, polychrome, polymorphous compost of life's customers, all the warm, mobile, noisy beings aquiver with urgent little desires and suddenly convulsed by fits of rage. In spring one rises up in revolt, quick sexual activity, one waves a gorgeous banner in 2014 as in 1982 as in 1848.

I have marched under seven wars threaded like gargantuan poison beads on the century's chain, I tell my daughter, one awaits the ashes of one disaster before sowing another in the neighboring field. If you consider humanity from the raised edge of the book, I tell her, you will see that it moves ponderously in an orderly succession of fires and carnages, I say, so that nobody misses a single one. Events, in Shakespeare's plays, happen one after another only so as to upset the soul's calculations, confuse the subject, test him with fear, disappointment, betrayal, forgetfulness, infidelity, by uprooting his heart, turning love inside out. Events are theater's subterfuges, I tell my daughter. What interests me in a play is not the battle and its causes, but how violent perturbations from without loose the winds of madness that blow through the dreamer's mental bedroom. So at one are we with our chains that we will die without ever having noticed our chronic state of captivity, unless by the happenstance of some earthquake. Tempests free us.

On Gay-Lussac and Ulm streets people stopped muttering and uttered long operatic screams, even Isaac, even Paul Celan. Oh the genius taste of dreams! People, rid of their bland white masks, shown for what they are: rosy, cashmere flesh-tinted faces, square jaws with yellow teeth, these youths have the power without the poetry and they gorge on powerless poets' hearts.

Nap. guards the entry and exit to every chapter in the young Henry Brulard's life, he keeps the motor purring, but my eyes are only for the adorations and the pains turned into stupefying sentences by the sufferer.

Wars erupt, peter out, wars take their place. Love remains, a pure enigma, a diamond endowed with words and silence. A diamond silence. A thousand fires and no explanation. It's like the Round Table Romance. All those knights, their swords, their reciprocal assassinations, for me the main thing is the kiss, for which one would give fifty years or one's life up to 2021.

64

It's not some Napoleon who fascinated me, I tell my daughter, but a sentence: "He went through life at a crazy speed." The sentence is a sphinx. The first time I read it I felt moved to tears, sure it was my explanation, my light, day dawning to the notes of a fanfare. I was dazzled. I didn't understand it, I admired it. It understands me, I was thinking, it's what is happening to me. The speed with which this cleanly articulated sentence shot through me stopped me seeing the *he*'s face. It was still him but some days he was another. The life and the speed, the life at the speed of this sentence allowed me to lift off effortlessly from myself. Outside I was inside, inside the outside. I murmur this sentence and right away I feel, again for the first time, the intoxication of feeling outside, in a wide open, cozy space, totally uninhabitable but *constituted* of crystallized speed.

This sentence existed in 68. *He* was Carlos. In no time *he* was Isaac. The same me, disassociated. Between 68 and this morning five minutes. At night I replay my life in a minute. In 68 it was January 20 for ever, I knew how to live life at high noon, and not just me. Him too, both of them, T. Thanks to cosmic and earthly events one suffered a painless detachment from life. I say: "in 68" as one says "in Illyria." I knew we were in an illusion. Sense of exultation. One is at time's *absolute*, it's the 20th. In a dream, a sentence flits past. Fast! Stop it. Speak! Who are you talking to? I jot the sibylline sentence down on a piece of paper on the low table near the fireplace at La Boucherie. Eat! I tell Los. It's for you. The winds ring out. It's for you. He turns it this way and that. Might he have written this sentence? Who is it? Whose? *Sa vie?* His life or hers? As a possessive "sa" is equivocal. Who lives what? – What. – Whose life? His life? Your life? My life? Is his life the other, the other's life? Life that a train speeds through? A plane? A dream? A love? So who is *he?* I don't know who it is. It can be an animated human *he* or an inanimate *it* animated by a movement imitated from nature. Maybe the wind?

Or maybe there's a person who lives his own life provided one separates the subject's-own-life from the subject, life as a track, a trail, a quarry, a lake, an airport, an arena, a forest, or maybe a tale?

What does a crazy speed mean? How can speed be crazy? When, when, what do you think?

He went through my life at a crazy speed, I tell my daughter. At that speed you feel everything like gods. You think at the speed of light: on the 20th it's the 8th already and the morning of the last act. The last act is the one with nobody in it.

One can be gods for an instant outside time but it can't last, I tell my daughter on the 27th. Surrounded by pines and their squirrels, we gaze at the gods' traces through the fanned-out branches.

A sombrero given to my son the reed. The little boy resembles a mushroom. My green sombrero, my son says. What did you do with it? I don't remember it was green, I say. A ghostly sombrero. He sees it. He was gentle. Sketched me with one stroke of his pencil. Had a real talent for drawing. True.

Those days Carlos went through life at a crazy speed. In order to go through your life you must be outside your life. He would don the fitted white suit to hold on tight for the passage apart from himself, relieved of the weight of his history. In this state, absolved, there is the lightning, one has it, one is it. I experienced this lightning on the 9th. Time no longer exists. That's what it did to me in 1948 and 1492.

– You are totally loco. Yes. You are a Spanish woman. A wild woman. You are Joana la Loca with her cadaver of a husband. You crisscross Spain in all directions year after year with a cadaver and at night you talk to him, you kiss him. Stop that. Last night I dreamed of you. I swam into all you and I went zoom along your spine. And I can tell you I met no cadaver. Quit talking to the dead.

He is reading Bram Stoker and he wonders why he has the urge to kill her. We are all necrophiliacs, aren't we?

On the 9th Los stayed in bed, apparently. As for me, I was on page [68], waking to the anguish of losing for ever the tie that makes me present in the world; finally I managed to pry my eyes open, already it was evening and I saw that I was looking at Isaac over his shoulder, I saw him waiting for me, his eternal, austere face, his piercing eyes, his basilisk gaze, his trembling confidence in the power of speech, and I saw that I was imagining us at the end of a long tumultuous century, seated on a wall warmed by a sun so constant so foreign to our insect affairs, a few meters from Montaigne's Tower, on the 10th. At that moment, with my life detached from me, I passed through it, I thought only of *him*. I was without consistency. I said "Yes." Not yes. "Yes."

Toward noon C. suggests we go and make a film on *The Castle* in Spain. I wanted to say: yes. *Oui*. The word sticks in my throat. As in *Macbeth*. My lips shape an O. At that moment, as in the film, I hear the door of the book slam. – Who is there, on page 32?? I answer. Then him, Isaac: – Is he handsome? – And you say? my daughter asks. – I answer, I say. At that moment, I say, *there is no one left* in the little bedroom. The interphone buzzes and, *as if I were there*, I hear his voice say: don't kill me. Or rather: as if I weren't there. –That's frightening, my daughter says.

I was trying to testify, I wanted to tell my daughter what was beyond me, I saw the scene clearly but my own absence of mass, my lack of self, paralyzed me. I was passing, I was past.

Letters. Ghosts they say. What a laugh. They are so much more alive than we poor humans, our tired beings, our perishable bodies.

I thought they'd stopped writing one another. But they go on, writing, talking, exchanging the news. When we forget they remember. That's why we brought them into the world, to free them from our deaths. What is it to them whether we agree or disagree?

Where? In numbered files. In boxes filthy as those goods trucks with immigrants hiding under their tarps, after they've crossed the planet.

A part of your soul that completely escapes you and is sealed: a supernatural kind of dream, kept safe, out of reach.

Under my name another.

His sweat his saliva his nails his shelves, classified and kept under lock and key in the Great Library. Secret sperm, in locked cupboards.

A piece of advice: don't reread the letters.

I won't. Have I ever read them?

Hesitation 1.

Hesitation 2.

Qualm 1: never. On pain of death?

and in that case never to know, death triumphs?

(Whereas he was life itself)

(A feeling: being the object of a spiteful accident, that's what death is, death in life)

Contrary uncertainties, brightly colored scenes, real laughs ringing out, one hears him in the distance, the struggle between all-that-was-good, charming, saved, happy, improvised, the courthouse is on holiday, carnival of baking hot days, slim arms, quiet paws swollen by their leaps and bounds, swaths of golden sand, the domes' gilt reduced to powder by the millenniums' slow bombardments; and all-that-has-not-been, followed by all-that-will-not-have-been, frightening hard anguished drowned, *if a clod be washed away by the sea, Europe is the less*, a climate of bad dreams, *for whom the bell tolls*, you know who, and no waking up.

A clod, a clod.

The last of the syllables, resists. Remains untranslatable. Does not want Nothing to gulp it down. Los

Qualm 2: murk of the end. After forty years of banishment the ghosts return. This is the truth.

A stool. I don't find the envelopes in the cardboard box.

Commentary: I didn't keep them. I dumped them into some cardboard box.

I find them

Then one morning, O sparkling Friday in spring a week after his death, I face the boxes like parcels of waves. Knocked down terrified splattered, I stagger out drowned. After the tempest of *The Tempest*, the voices. Oh, there's no drowning the voices. Set free from the old bodies, vigorous, light, voluble, a thousand things to recount.

Found: sheets of onion skin reporting a fateful night. Garish light effects, genius naturally unaware of itself, innocence, fatality, Neccessity Anankhe walks the streets of the great cities Amorkroywennilrebsirap

This self of mine is utterly oblivious of such deeds. She who was me what to call her? No subject pronoun fits. She is someone who bears witness in detail and precisely. The obsessive precision of dreams eager to prove they are more real than reality. So it was a dream? A tale? A report without the least hesitation, addressed to nobody.

It's the she I have left or who has left me, me, therefore me, this me of this month, I swear, I can't answer for her. She never dreamed I would take her place.

Radical discontinuity, I have been others. Don't call me *you* in the singular. Still, the writing, the syntax, her sentences, her untrembling acuity are yours.

Not mine.

Look! In English: her letters. Mine? Sleeping in the Foreign Library. Strange foreign detachment. Perhaps in English too?

We loved one another in English?

– It is also a way of preserving something, my daughter says. – What! I exclaim. Preserving the love of the love? I don't speak this thought out loud, I don't think it.

– Independently of sexual differences, my daughter says. It's part of the story's charm. One more playful element, another kind of freedom. My daughter says. When one is in the other language.

– Hello my love! How goes it?

– Lieberty, I say. My love is in your language.

I only loved Isaac in French.

I only ever *loved* in French

I love you in the night Mister Tyger Tyger.

You can only say *longtemps* in French, I say.

In English *longtemps* is short.

Say whatever you like to say but don't stick to it.

Don't stick. I pick up *his scissors* and I cut. I am cut.

We hadn't seen each other in a while. It was a day like other days, torrential, gay. We were laughing. We were striding across dunes. He pointed out some big sandpits and said we should slide down into them one day, it's lots of fun, no time now, keep it for next time. The end is in sight. We rush back at a crazy speed. At the speed of life and death. C., going faster and faster, sticks out his tongue. I take it in my mouth. At first I didn't like the English then I recognized the taste, the cadence, no man is an island and we covered a dozen meters in a single kiss. I had to go, quickly I gathered up my papers. C. gave me two small volumes printed on onion skin: his last volumes of poetry. Suddenly I shuddered. Isaac! I got back much later than I'd said. I was wearing heels, not the most practical, I dropped my sneakers, and other things too, the race was on, I'll be back, I rushed for the exit, in my haste and without asking any questions I retraced the path of the apocalyptic flight on page 150 of *Wuthering Heights*. In my flight through the kitchen I knocked over Hareton who was hanging a litter of puppies from a chair-back in the doorway of *Zone Sacrée* I saw the five little puppies dangling, and like an escaped soul, I bounded, leaped and flew down the steep road then shot direct across the moor rolling over banks and wading through marshes

It was quite something all the same. I ran. See you soon Carlos, we'll talk.

Already the book. Only a few pages long. It's that I'm not writing it. – A ten-page book? My publisher is enthusiastic.

Overnight I add a chapter in which I play the lamb with the Tiger. On the 26th I can't find the Dream. A fateful loss. As if I'd been condemned to repeat the test of losing Carlos. A perpetual loss. Lost: even the dreams.

In place of the lost dream, where I thought I'd left it, on my table – and it's not under the cats either – I find: the scissors.

They took everything, death. Except for the pair of mustache scissors.

– I cannot stop worrying about which tense to use, I tell my daughter. I could not write: He went through life at a crazy speed. This life, this passage, this speed, this craziness didn't want me to talk about them in the tenses of dreams. These events have a literary will of their own, I sense. A desire for immortalization. They require a present. The present, which present? So many of them, that present themselves, that pass. The past remains past.

On the 27th *I passed into the present.*

Donne's present. It tolls for me. The present tolls.

Another End! In short, after a whole summer spent in the revenant days, I *want* to forget.

– Do you remember, I ask the children, our apartment on the Rue Lhomond?

– The sombrero, my son says, I'd hear the somber hero.

– ... and all the rest, my daughter says.

We were traversed unawares by Flaubert's humor one Wednesday in 1876. How time flies, Isaac thinks. Tiny little hundreds of years. Ah! ...

THANKS TO

William Black – Emily Brontë – Georg Büchner
– Hernán Cortés – John Donne – Jakob Lenz – Ovid –
Marcel Proust – William Shakespeare – Stendhal

TRANSLATOR'S NOTES

I wish to thank Hélène Cixous for her comments and suggestions on the translation-in-progress. Any errors of omission or commission are, of course, my responsibility.

who it is, kill (page 1): as a response to the sounds of the French phrase, *qui l'est*, that precedes it.

to kill to tell (page 1): in French, *pour le pire pour le dire*, a play on sound.

***nors, Tongue nor heart* (page 1):** in English in the original.

The hour lures (page 2): in French, *l'heure leurre*.

sly dry threadbare silence (page 2): *silence éliminé rusé usé*.

If death knocked, she ... (page 3): death, *la mort*, is feminine in French.

When love … flow (page 6): John Donne, "The Ecstasy." In English in the original.

Tongue nor heart Cannot conceive (page 7): Macbeth Act II, Scene 3. In English in the original, along with other words and phrases in the same paragraph.

My love; Your Los; *The Book of Los; The Book of Loss; The Book of Los* (pages 7–8): all in English in the original.

Do help me, love (page 8): in English in the original.

a violet pansy (page 9): *pensée*, which can mean "pansy" or "thought" in French.

the naked blow from the blue (page 9): in French *le coup nu venu des nues*, with three rhymes and a play on *nu* ("naked") and *nues* ("clouds").

Second floor (page 9): or, in the United States, the third floor.

He's a genius … fulfilled (page 18): in English in the original.

cothurnuses (page 18): High Greek or Roman shoe, laced up; also thick-soled shoe worn by actors in a tragedy in order to appear more majestic and imposing.

Carlos died yesterday (page 18): in English in the original.

cries-laughs, the crilaughs (page 18): in French *cris-rires … crires*.

Kill me … mere man (page 19): in English in the original, by way of John Donne's "The Damp."

mysterious or mister (page 20): "mister" in English in the original.

earnest or giggly (page 20): *Mimi a l'air perpétuellement sérieux ou rieuse*, playing on gender ambiguities.

good and male (page 22): *au-delà du bien et du mâle*, a play on the sounds of *mal* (evil) and *mâle* (male). Also an allusion to Nietzsche's *Beyond Good and Evil*.

Call me Ishmael; Call me Los (page 22): in English in the original.

myriad-minded (page 23): in English in the original.

Each ... ass **(page 23):** in English in the original.

Tyger Burning: Bird, Blueblack Bird (page 28): in English in the original.

For they ... the time **(page 30):** in English in the original. A quotation from *Hamlet*, Act II, Scene 2 (cf. also opening epigraph).

I'll have him, and tonight laurel (page 31): in French *aujourd'hui je l'aurais, et cette nuit laurier*, a play on the similar sounds of *je l'aurais* and *laurier* as well as on Daphne's transformation.

Why ... not sweet (page 32): in English in the original.

burning bright (page 32): in English in the original.

in the forests of the night (page 32): in English in the original.

what shoulder ... heart (page 32): in English in the original.

and what ... dread feet (page 32): in English in the original.

Please mister Tyger! (page 33): in English in the original.

please big mister Tyger (page 33): in English in the original.

Did he ... make thee (page 33): in English in the original.

Tell me tell (page 35): in English in the original.

It tolls for thee (page 36): in English in the original (cf. John Donne, "Meditation XVII").

"one of the fine arts" (page 39): an allusion to De Quincey's essay "On Murder Considered as One of the Fine Arts."

its marrow, its hair, his secrets (page 39): in French *ses* could be either "his" or "its." HC (conversation, December 2014) favored keeping the ambiguity in English by using a mixture of masculine and neuter possessive pronouns.

Hello ... goldeng- (page 41): in English in the original.

I seem ... 2968 outside (page 42): in English in the original.

I am forty (page 48): in English in the original.

Why ... Des astres, non? (page 48): mostly in English in the original. *Des astres* – in French, the phrase is *Dix astres* ("ten stars"), playing with the sound of the French word *désastre*.

***My man of men* (pages 52–3):** in English in the original.

***You castrating bitch* (page 57):** in English in the original.

the world bounded ... bonded ... boner (page 60): in French *le monde a bondé sur le quai. Bandé? Bondi*, playing on the sounds of *bonder* ("to fill"), *bander* ("have an erection"), and *bondir* ("bound").

***To outhamlet ... jesus* (page 61):** in English in the original.

***Café la Bucherie* (page 61):** *café La Boucherie* in the text, playing on the sounds of *bûche* (log) and *bouche* (mouth). Café la Bucherie – after an old Parisian port where logs were unloaded – is in the Fifth Arrondissement, on the Seine opposite Notre Dame. The English bookstore

81

Shakespeare and Company is located at 37 Rue de la Bûcherie. Its original, at 12 Rue de l'Odéon in the Sixth Arrondissement, published Joyce's *Ulysses* in 1922.

Calderón (page 62): Pedro Calderón de la Barca, author of *Life is a Dream* (1635).

"He went through life at a crazy speed" (page 65): *Il traversait sa vie à une vitesse folle.* An allusion to the opening sentence of Georg Büchner's *Lenz* (1839): "On January 20, Lenz went walking through the mountains," as well as to Paul Celan's "Conversation in the Mountains."

"Might he have written this sentence? Who is it?" (page 66): in French, the word *phrase* ("sentence") is feminine in gender, so the question *Qui est elle?* suggests both "Who is it?" and "Who is she?" leading to some word play, here and in the following lines.

Stop that ... cadaver (page 67): in English in the original.

I said "Yes." Not yes. "Yes." (page 68): the difference is one of intonation. "Yes" is spoken, with the emphasis of something said out loud (HC, conversation, February 5, 2015).

***if a clod ... less; for whom the bell tolls; A clod, a clod* (page 70):** in English in the original (cf. John Donne, "Meditation XVII").

this me of this month (page 71): in French, *ce moi de ce mois-ci.*

Hello my love! (page 72): in English in the original.

Lieberty (page 72): in French, *Lieberté* a mixture of German *liebe* ("to love") and the French *liberté*.

I love you ... Tyger (page 72): in English in the original.

Say whatever … stick to it. … Don't stick (page 72): in English in the original.

no man is an island (page 73): in English in the original (cf. John Donne, "Meditation XVII").

In my flight … doorway (page 73): in English in the original (cf. Emily Brontë, *Wuthering Heights*).

I bounded … marshes (page 73): in English in the original (cf. Emily Brontë, *Wuthering Heights*).

It tolls for me (page 75): in English in the original (cf. John Donne, "Meditation XVII").